By Sabrina Mesko

HEALING MUDRAS
Yoga for Your Hands
Random House - Original edition

POWER MUDRAS
Yoga Hand Postures for Women
Random House - Original edition

MUDRA - Gestures of POWER
DVD - Sounds True

CHAKRA MUDRAS DVD set
HAND YOGA for Vitality, Creativity and Success
HAND YOGA for Concentration, Love and Longevity

HEALING MUDRAS
Yoga for Your Hands - New Edition

HEALING MUDRAS - New Edition in full color:
Healing Mudras I. ~ For Your Body
Healing Mudras II. ~ For Your Mind
Healing Mudras III. ~ For Your Soul

POWER MUDRAS
Yoga Hand Postures for Women - New Edition

MUDRA THERAPY
Hand Yoga for Pain Management and Conquering Illness

YOGA MIND
45 Meditations for Inner Peace, Prosperity and Protection

MUDRAS for ASTROLOGICAL SIGNS
Volumes I. ~ XII.
MUDRAS for ARIES, TAURUS, GEMINI, CANCER, LEO, VIRGO,
LIBRA, SCORPIO, SAGITTARIUS, CAPRICORN, AQUARIUS, PISCES
12 Book Series

LOVE MUDRAS
Hand Yoga for Two

MUDRAS AND CRYSTALS
The Alchemy of Energy Protection

THE HOLISTIC CAREGIVER
A Guidebook for at-home care in late stage of Alzheimer's and dementia

MUDRAS

for

LEO

By Sabrina Mesko Ph.D.H.

The material contained in this book has been written for informational purposes and is not intended as a substitute for medical advice nor is it intended to diagnose, treat, cure, or prevent disease. If you have a medical issue or illness, consult a qualified physician.

A Mudra Hands™ Book
Published by Mudra Hands Publishing

Copyright © 2013 Sabrina Mesko Ph.D.H.

Photography by Mara
Animal photography by Sabrina Mesko
Illustrations by Kiar Mesko
Cover photo by Mara

Printed in the United States of America

ISBN-13:978-0615920900
ISBN-10:061592090X

For all my Leo Friends

TABLE OF CONTENTS

THE MUDRA PRACTICE IS A
COMPLIMENTARY HEALING TECHNIQUE,
THAT OFFERS FAST AND EFFECTIVE
POSITIVE RESULTS.

MUDRAS WORK HARMONIOUSLY
WITH OTHER TRADITIONAL,
ALTERNATIVE AND COMPLEMENTARY
HEALING PROTOCOLS.

THEY HELP RESTORE DEPLETED
SUBTLE ENERGY STATES
AND OPTIMIZE THE PRACTITIONER'S
OVERALL STATE OF WELLNESS.

Mudras for LEO

JULY 23 - AUGUST 23

BODY
Heart, spine, back

PLANET
Sun

COLORS
all colors of the sun

ELEMENT
Fire

STONES and GEMS
Gold, Ruby

ANIMAL
Cats

Introduction

Ever since I can remember, I have been fascinated by the never ending view of the stars in the sky and the presence of other mysterious planets. As a child I wondered for hours about where does the Universe end and when my Father explained the possibility that time and space exist in a very different way than we imagined, my mind went wild with possibilities. I was however quite skeptical about astrology in general until one day in my early youth, a dear friend introduced me to a true Master of Vedic Astrology. He quickly and completely diminished any of my doubts about how precise certain facts can be revealed in one's Celestial map.

It was as if an invisible veil had been removed, and I was granted a peek over to the other side. The astrologer also adamantly pointed out that nothing is written in stone and one's destiny has a lot of space to navigate thru. You can make the best of the situation if you know your given parameters. My fascination and use of astrological science continues to this day and compliments and enriches my work with other observation techniques that I use when consulting.

One is born with character aspects and potential for realization of mapped-out future events, but there is always a possibility that another road may be taken. This has to do with the choices we make. Free will is given to all of us, even though often the choices we have seem to be very limited. But still, the choices are always there, forcing us to consciously participate and eventually take responsibility for our decisions, actions, and consequences.

The science of Astrology has been around for millenniums and even though some people are still doubtful, I always remind them that there is no disputing the fact, that the Moon affects the high and low tide of our Oceans - hence our bodies consisting mostly of water are affected by planetary movements in many fascinating and profound ways. Even the biggest skeptic agrees with that fact.

The Love of the Universal Power for each one of us is unconditional, everlasting and omnipresent. No matter what kind of life-journey you have, it is the very best one designed especially for you, rest assured. And when you are experiencing life's various challenges and wishing for a smooth ride instead, keep in mind that a life filled with lessons is a life fulfilling its purpose. The tests you encounter in your daily life are your opportunities. The wisdom learned is your asset, and the experiences gained are your wealth. Your Spirit's abundance is measured by the battles you fought and how you fought them. Did you help others and leave this world a better place in any way? Your true intention matters more than you know.

Each one of us has a very unique-one of a kind celestial map placed gently, but firmly and irrevocably into effect at the precise time of our birth. There are certain aspects of one's chart that reveal possible character tendencies and predisposed behavior in regards to love, partnerships, maintaining one's health, pursuit of success and a way of communicating. The benefits of knowing and understanding the effects of your chart on various aspects of your life can be profound. It can help you understand and prepare ahead of time for certain circumstances that are coming your way, which increases the possibility of a better quality of life in general.

If you knew that a specific time period could be beneficial for your career wouldn't it be good to know that ahead of your plans? If you are aware that certain aspects of your physical constitution are predisposed to a weakness or sensitivity, wouldn't it be beneficial to pay attention and prevent a possible future health ailment?

If you can foresee that a certain time will be slower for you in achieving positive results, wouldn't it be wise to use that time for preparation for a more fortuitous timing? How many times have you attempted to pursue a dream of yours that just didn't seem to want to happen? And when you were completely exhausted and disillusioned, the fortunate opportunity presented itself, except now you were tired, overwhelmed and had no energy or enthusiasm left. Having such information ahead of time would offer you the chance to save your energy during quiet, less active time, so that when your luck is more likely, you can seize the opportunity and make the most of it. Since writing my first books on Mudras a while ago, my work has expanded into many different areas, however I always included Mudras into my new ventures. When I designed International Wellness and Spa centers, I included Mudra programs to share these beneficial techniques with a wide audience. I included Mudras into my weekly TV show and guided large audiences thru practice on live shows.

Mudras will forever fascinate me and I have been humbled and excited how many practitioners from around the world have written me, grateful to have these techniques and most importantly really experiencing positive effects in time of need. Therefore it has been a natural idea for me to combine these two of my favorite topics and create a series of Mudra sets for all twelve Astrological signs.

The Mudras depicted in this book are specifically selected for the astrological sign of Aries with intention to help you maximize your gifts and soften the challenges that your celestial map contains.

It is important to know that each astrological chart - celestial map-contains information that can be used beneficially and there are no "bad signs" or "better sings". Your chart is unique as are you. By gaining information, knowledge and understanding what the placements of the planets offer you, your path to self knowledge is strengthened.

I hope this book will attract astrology readers as well as meditation and yoga practitioners and help you utilize the beneficial combination of both these fascinating techniques. Knowledge will help you experience the very best possible version of your life. The biggest mystery in your life is You. Discover who you are and enjoy the journey.

And remember, no matter what life presents you with, don't forget to smile and keep a happy heart. With each experience gained you are spiritually wealthier for it. And that my friend, stays with you forever.

The wisdom gained is eternally imprinted in your soul.

Blessings,

Sabrina

MUDRAS

Mudras are movements involving only fingers, hands and arms. Mudras originated in ancient Egypt where they were practiced by high priests and priestesses in sacred rituals. Mudras can be found in every culture of the world. We all use Mudras in our everyday life when gesturing while communicating and when holding our hands in various intuitive positions. Mudras used in yoga practice offer great benefits and have a tremendously positive overall effect on our overall state of well-being. By connecting specific fingertips and your palms in various Mudra positions, you are directly affecting complex energy currents of your subtle energy body. As numerous energy currents run thru your brain centers, Mudras help stimulate specific areas for an overall state of emotional, physical and mental well being.

INSTRUCTIONS FOR MUDRA PRACTICE

YOUR BODY POSTURE
During the Mudra practice sit in an upright position with a straight spine, with both your feet on the ground or in a cross legged position. Comfort is essential so that you may practice undisturbed and focus on proper practice positions.

YOUR EYES
Keep your eyes closed and gently lightly lift the gaze above the horizon.

WHERE
For achieving best results of ideal Mudra practice it is essential that you find a peaceful place, without distractions. Once your Mudra practice is established, you can practice Mudras anywhere.

WHEN
You may practice Mudras at any time. Best times for practice are first thing in the morning and at bedtime. Avoid practicing Mudras on a full stomach, and after a big meal wait for an hour before practice.

HOW LONG
Each Mudra should be practiced for at least 3 minutes at a time. Ideal practice is 3 Mudras for 3 minutes each with a follow up short 3 minutes of complete stillness, peace and meditation or reflection.

HOW OFTEN
You may practice Mudras every day. Explore various Mudras by selecting a Mudra that fits your specific needs for any given day.

BREATH CONTROL
Proper breathing is essential for optimal Mudra practice. There are two main breathing techniques that can be used with your practice.

LONG DEEP SLOW BREATH
Slowly and deeply inhale thru your nose while relaxing and expanding the area or your solar plexus and lower stomach. Exhale thru the nose slowly while gently contracting the stomach area and pulling your stomach in. Pace your breathing slowly and notice the immediate calming effects. This breathing technique is appropriate for relaxation, inducing calmness and peace.

BREATH OF FIRE
Inhale and exhale thru the nose at a much faster pace while practicing the same concept of expanding navel area and contracting with each exhalation. Unless otherwise noted Mudras are generally practiced with the long slow breath.The breath of fire has an energizing, recharging effect on body and is to be used only when so noted.

CHAKRAS

Along our spine, starting at the base and continuing up towards the top of your head, lie subtle energy centers-vortexes-called charkas, that have a powerful effect on the overall state of your health and well being.

The practice of Mudras profoundly affects the proper function of these energy centers and magnifies their power.

Our subtle energy body is highly sensitive to outside sensory stimuli of sound, aromas, visuals and outside electric currents that constantly surround us. Frequencies that permeate specific locations may attract or bother you. Perhaps you may feel eager to stay somewhere where the energy suits you and yet feel suffocated when the environment does not agree with you. We are all sensitive to energies, but some of us feel them more than others.

A positive blend of energies with another person can create a magnet-like effect, whereas another person's negative unharmonious subtle energy field subconsciously pushes you away.

By leading healthy lives and optimizing the proper function of charkas, you empower your subtle energy bodies adding strength to your physical body, mind and spirit. Destructive behavior like addictions and abuse weakens your Auric field and "leaks" your vital energy. By maintaining a healthy Aura-energy field, you can fine-tune your natural capacity for "sensing" places, situations and people that compliment your energy frequency.

In a state of "clean energy" you achieve capacity for high awareness and become your own best guide.

CHAKRAS IN THE BODY

Base Chakra: Foundation
Second Chakra: Sexuality
Third Chakra: Ego
Fourth Chakra: Love
Fifth Chakra: Truth
Sixth Chakra: Intuition
Seventh Chakra: Divine Wisdom

FIRST CHAKRA
LOCATION: Base of the spine
GLAND: Gonad
COLOR: Red
REPRESENTS:
Foundation, shelter, survival,
courage, inner security, vitality

SECOND CHAKRA
LOCATION: Sex organs
GLAND: Adrenal
COLOR: Orange
REPRESENTS:
Creative expression, sexuality,
procreation, family

THIRD CHAKRA
LOCATION: Solar plexus
GLAND: Pancreas
COLOR: Yellow
REPRESENTS:
Ego, intellect, emotions of fear and anger

FOURTH CHAKRA
LOCATION: Heart
GLAND: Thymus
COLOR: Green
REPRESENTS:
All matters of the heart, love,
self–love, compassion and faith

FIFTH CHAKRA
LOCATION: Throat
GLAND: Thyroid
COLOR: Blue
REPRESENTS:
Communication, truth,
higher knowledge, your voice

SIXTH CHAKRA
LOCATION: Third Eye
GLAND: Pineal
COLOR: Indigo
REPRESENTS:
Intuition, inner vision, the Third eye

SEVENTH CHAKRA
LOCATION: Top of the head - Crown
GLAND: Pituitary
COLOR: White and Violet
REPRESENTS:
The universal God consciousness,
the heavens, unity

NADIS

Your subtle energy body contains an amazing network of electric currents called Nadis. There are 72.000 energy currents that run throughout your body from toes to the top of your head as well as your fingertips. These channels of light must be clear and vibrant with life force for your optimal health and empowerment. With regular Mudra practice you can open, clear, reactivate and re-energize your energy currents.

Your Hands and Fingers

While practicing Mudras you are magnifying the effects of the Solar system on your physical, mental and spiritual body. Each finger is influenced by the following planets:

THE THUMB - MARS

THE INDEX FINGER - JUPITER

THE MIDDLE FINGER - SATURN

THE RING FINGER – THE SUN

THE LITTLE FINGER - MERCURY

MANTRA

Combining the Mudra practice with appropriate Mantras magnifies the beneficial effects of these ancient self-healing techniques.

The hard palate in your mouth has 58 energy meridian points that connect to and affect your entire body.

By singing, speaking or whispering Mantras, you touch these energy points in a specific order that is beneficial and has a harmonious and healing effect on your physical, mental and spiritual state.

The ancient science of Mantras helps you reactivate nadis, magnifies and empowers your energy field, improves your concentration and stills your mind.

About Astrology

The word Horoscope originates from a Latin word ORA–hour and SCOPOS–view. One could presume that Horoscope means "a look into your hour of birth". The precise moment of your birth determines your celestial set-up.

An accurate astrological chart can reveal most detailed aspects of your life, your character, your gifts, your future possible events, challenges that await you, lucky events that are bestowed upon you, and your outlook for happy relationships, successful careers, accomplishments, health and many possible variations of life events. I say possible, because your decisions will determine the outcome.

There are 12 signs in the Zodiac and your birth-day reflects the position of your Sun sign. The specific positions of other planets in your chart are calculated considering the precise moment-hour and minute and of course location of your birth. The birth time will reveal your Rising or Ascending sign, which will further determine other essential facts of your chart.

The constant transitional movements of the Planets affect each one of us differently, a time that may be difficult for some may prove supremely lucky for another and yet we are interconnected by mutual effects of continuous planetary movements. Nothing is standing still, the changes are ongoing. On a different note, a few slow moving planets connect us in other ways, as they keep certain generations under specific aspects and influences. We are all inseparable and in continuous motion.

There are numerous fascinating ways to use astrology and there is no doubt that the constant motion of all these powerful and majestic Planets in our Solar system affect each and every one of us differently. Astrology can be used as an additional tool to help you continue progressing on the mysterious life journey of self discovery and self-realization.

Remember, the power of decision is yours as is the responsibility for consequences. Make peace with your doubts, pursue your dreams and relish in results.

When the outcome is less than what you expected, learn to pick yourself up and continue on, wiser with knowledge you gained, that alone being a good reason for remaining optimistic. When the outcome surpasses your expectations, well, then you will know what to do…mostly take a breath, smile, and enjoy the moment.

YOUR SUN SIGN

There are 12 signs in the Zodiac. The day of your birth determines your Sun-sign. Most often this is the extent of average person's knowledge and interest in astrology. However, the other aspects in the astrological chart are equally as important and need to be taken into consideration. In this book your main guide is your Sun sign's dispositions, tendencies, weaknesses and gifts. Certainly there are endless combinations of charts and your Sun sign alone will not reveal the complete picture of your celestial map.

For more detailed information and reflection about your chart, you need to know your ascending-rising sign.

YOUR ASCENDING-RISING SIGN

Your rising sign, also known as the ascendant, reflects the degree of ecliptic rising over the eastern horizon at the precise moment of your birth. It reveals the foundation of your personality. That means that even if you have the same birthday with someone else, your time of birth would create completely different aspects and influences in your chart. No two people are alike. You are one of a kind and so is everyone else. However, you may have some strong similarities and timing aspects that will be often alike. Your rising sign also reveals the basis of your chart and House placements. Your rising sign determines and is in your first house. There are 12 Houses and each depicts precise in-depth information about all aspects of your physical life, emotional make and character tendencies. It is incredibly complex and fascinating. Regarding your Mudra practice in combination with your Astrological Sign, it would be beneficial to know also your Rising sign and apply Mudras that empower your Rising sign as well. For example; if your Sun sign is Aries, but your rising sign is Libra-it would be most beneficial to practice Mudra sets for both signs.

HOW TO USE THIS BOOK

In each book of the *Mudras for the Astrological Signs* series, you will find Mudras for different astrological signs that will help you in most important areas of your life: Health, Love, Success, and Overcoming your challenging qualities. We all have them, as we also all have gifts. This book is specific for the sign of Aries. You may change your Mudra practice daily as needed, and keep in mind, that certain habits or tendencies need a longer time to adjust, change, and improve. Be patient, kind, and loving towards yourself.

Mudras for Transcending Challenges

Each one of us has a few character tendencies or weaknesses that are connected to our astrological chart. To help you transcend, overcome and redirect these challenges into your beneficial assets, you can use the Mudras in this chapter.

Mudras for Health and Beauty

Each astrological sign rules certain areas of your body. The Mudras in this chapter will help you strengthen your physical weaknesses while maintaining a healthy body, and a beautiful, vibrant appearance.

Mudras for Love

The Mudras in this chapter will help you understand your love temperament, your expectations, your longings and how to attract the optimal love partner into your life. It is most beneficial to know how others perceive you in the matters of the heart. It will also help you understand your partner and their astrologically influenced love map.

Mudras for Success

The Mudras in this chapter will offer you tools to present yourself to the world in your optimal light. Often one is confused in which direction to turn or where their strength lies. Mudras will help you focus and remember your essential creative desires, help you gain self-confidence and inner security to recognize your desired and destined path. If you know what you want, and your purpose is harmonious for the better good of all, your success is within reach.

MUDRAS *for* TRANSCENDING CHALLENGES

MUDRA FOR
RECEIVING GOD'S LAW

You are strong, powerful and as the "King of the Jungle" you have a hint of a bossy streak. Your opinions are heard and your enthusiastic, warm-hearted nature is present in everything you touch. But when you are such a self-assured leader, sometimes the responsibility that comes along with the territory can cramp your free creative spirit. It is a good time to remember that there is a higher power than yourself, that actually plays the larger, decisive role in everyone's life. Remaining open to that Universal power and understanding that your gifted artistic nature is a direct result of God's generosity, it is wise to consciously reconnect with it, and show humble respect while continuously increasing your receptivity and wealth of talents.

CHAKRA: 7

COLOR: Violet

MANTRA:

OM

(God in His Absolute State)

Sit with a straight back. Lift the right hand to heart level, palm facing down, and the left hand to your solar plexus area, palm facing up towards the sky. Leave enough space between the palms for a small ball. Elbows are to the side. All fingers are together and straight. Hold the Mudra and concentrate on the energy between your palms.

BREATH: Long, deep and slow.

MUDRA FOR READJUSTING YOUR PERCEPTION

You are generous and loving in nature, however you dislike interference or disobedience in regards to your opinions or rules. And yet, the best leaders know their people and the land, and are capable of seeing the world from many points of view. This Mudra will help strengthen this capacity in you, so that you may be able to adjust and improve your leading tendencies while truly understanding the needs and situations of others. This way, others will trust your guiding powers even more, and together you can create a powerful and harmonious empire.

CHAKRA : 6, 7

COLOR: Indigo, violet

MANTRA:

SA TA NA MA
(Infinity, Birth, Death, Rebirth)

Sit with a straight back. Make circles with the thumbs and index fingers and spread out the rest of the fingers. Lift your arms so your elbows are perpendicular to the ground and your hands are at eye level. Now move your hands toward each other until you can look through the openings of your fingers. As you separate your hands, take a long, slow inhale. As you bring them together in front of your face, exhale, long, deep, and slow. Observe the change of perception with the movement of your hands.

BREATH: Long inhale when hands apart, long exhale when moving hands together.

MUDRA FOR
INNER INTEGRITY

For all the power and capacity to be the center of the Universe, it is interesting that after all, you are very sensitive and can be easily hurt. This will often involve your pride, which is healthy in small portions and under certain circumstances, but do not let it come in your way of reaching your goal. You can stay true to yourself and be happily fulfilled. How to keep that inner integrity and maintain a balance with everything you are doing? Practice this Mudra to find that inner balance and empower the capacity to clearly sense what feels and is the right thing to do or say in any circumstance. With power comes responsibility - wear it well and you will impress all, including yourself.

CHAKRA: 4

COLOR: Green

Sit with a straight back. Bend your elbows and lift your upper arms parallel to the ground. Bring your hands to ear level, palms facing out. Curl the fingers inward and point the thumbs out toward your ears. Hold for three minutes and relax.

BREATH: Short, fast, breath of fire from the navel.

MUDRAS
for HEALTH
and BEAUTY

MUDRA FOR HEALTHY BREAST AND HEART

Taking care of your heart is essential and that means in all aspects and areas. A healthy diet, and physical activity to keep the stamina is important. However, your enthusiasm can sometimes prevent you from remembering where your limitations are. You do need to rest and take a break and no matter how fiery your creative spell is, take a breather so you can   return invigorated and recharged.This Mudra is excellent for keeping your heart and breast healthy and filled with fresh vital energy, working at optimal capacity.

CHAKRA: 4

COLOR: Green

Sit with a straight back. Relax your arms at your sides with the palms facing forward. Then alternatively bend each elbow so that the forearms come toward the heart center as rapidly as possible. When your right hand is at your chest, the left hand is away from the body and when the left hand is at your chest, the right hand is away from the body. Do not bend the wrists or hands and do not touch the chest. Practice at a rapid pace four times while you inhale, four times while you exhale, until you feel hot, then relax for a few minutes.

BREATH: Long, deep and slow with motions as described.

MUDRA for
Activating Lower CHAKRAS

Your back and spine need attention and proper care. A healthy spine affects your entire mental and emotional disposition, as well as the level of physical strength and endurance. With regular exercise and care, it can be the pillar of your strength and overall health. For a strong and recharged base and lower spine, practice this Mudra and help keep it clear of stuck energy, always recharged and healthy.

CHAKRA : 1, 2

COLOR: Red, orange

MANTRA:
SAT NAM
(Truth is God's name, One in Spirit)

Sit with a straight back. Place both hands at waist level, thumbs open with palms facing down. All fingers are stretched and together, the tips of the middle fingers an inch apart. As you inhale, concentrate on expanding the lower area of your stomach. When you exhale, contract the stomach and bring your fingertips closer until they almost touch. Concentrate on bringing vital creative energy into that area of your body, filling it with life force.

BREATH: Start slowly and after a minute increase the tempo into the breath of fire, after a minute slow down and return to the slow, deep breath.

MUDRA FOR
MIDDLE SPINE

Keeping your heart healthy reflects also in care for you middle spine-your center of power. Proper breathing is your essential tool for maintaining optimal balance and harmony in that region. Make it a regular habit and dedicate every day a few minutes of your time to this Mudra practice. Truly focus with your mind on recharging and revitalizing your center. This way, your creative ideas will have a proper chance to come to fruition, so you can be happy, fulfilled and can share your inspiring loving nature with others.

CHAKRA : 3, 4

COLOR: Yellow, Green

MANTRA:
OM
(God in His Absolute State)

Sit with and place your fists on your knees or in front of you with elbows bent. Leave the thumbs pointing up. Concentrate on your thumbs, sending healing energy to the middle area of your back. Keep the thumbs stretched and hold for three minutes.

BREATH: Long, deep and slow.

MUDRAS
for LOVE

MUDRA for Opening Your HEART

Everyone loves a strong and self-assured partner, but make sure that your strength does not develop into an overly domineering disposition. It is perfectly fine to be vulnerable and it is also very acceptable that you are not always right about everything you say or do. Strength also comes in acceptance of one's weakness and not let pride prevent you from enjoying a healthy and fulfilling love relationship. And yet, with your other side of extreme and quick sensitivity, it is a good idea to take a few minutes, get centered and truly open your heart to your lover. Juts relax and be, no need to be the unbeatable leader every second of the day. Let your lover feel an equal partner and play fair. It will be much more fun.

CHAKRA : 4

COLOR: Green

MANTRA:
SAT NAM
(Truth is God's Name, One in Spirit)

Sit with a straight spine and lift your hands in front of your heart with palms and fingers open as if creating a cup. Keep all the fingers stretched and feel healing energy pouring into your fingertips and the area of your heart.

BREATH: Long, deep and slow.

MUDRA FOR COMPASSION

You are quite the idealist in love aspects and sometimes that can be an impossibly demanding role for your partner. Nobody is perfect and when you suddenly realize that is a fact, be gentle and kind. Expand your heart in compassion and truly make an effort to understand your lover. Give them some air and let them find their own voice or individualism. And then a magical thing will happen-you will fall in love with them even more - perhaps again idealizing them in a different context. In either case, expanding your capacity to love unconditionally by accepting one as they are, will alleviate your unreasonable disappointment and you will experience profound love on a whole different level, perhaps even better.

CHAKRA : 4

COLOR: Green

MANTRA:
AKAL AKAL SIRI AKAL
(Timeless Is the One Who Achieves
Perfection of the Spirit)

Sit with a straight spine. Extend your arms out to the sides parallel to the ground with the palms turned front. Stretch out the fingers and hold them still. Turn your head to the right side and back to the center four times, then to the left side and back to the center four times. Continue for a few minutes and concentrate on your heart center. Become aware of the energy in your palms.

BREATH: Inhale long once as you move your head to the right, and exhale long once you move your head back to center. Repeat four times to each side. Relax and sit still for a few minutes.

MUDRA FOR
UPLIFTING YOUR HEART

Being overly sensitive is a weakness that does not bring you much joy. Sulking over an unimportant detail, event or spoken word, is best released and forgotten. Concentrate on the happy aspects and allow your naturally sunny disposition to shine thru the unnecessary clouds of your temporary gloomy mood. When you are in need to overcome this tendency, practice this Mudra and instantly uplift your heart and general outlook. Sunny days filled with love lay ahead. Your partner will be overjoyed to have you back.

CHAKRA : 4

COLOR: Green

Sit with a straight back, and lift up your arms shoulder level, elbows bent and parallel to the ground. Tuck your thumbs under your armpits and keep the rest of your fingers straight and together. Your hands should be above your breasts, palms facing down. As you inhale, the distance between the middle fingertips gets bigger; as you exhale, the middle fingertips should touch or cross each other. With each inhalation feel the healing energy expand your heart and chest area. Continue for three minutes and relax.

BREATH: Long, deep and slow.

MUDRAS
for SUCCESS

MUDRA FOR
MENTAL BALANCE

When you have a clear vision of your mission, nothing will stand in your way. However, more often than not, in order to realize your dream, you have to work with others and need to compromise a bit. This can present an obstacle and be very frustrating for you. Keep the eye on the ball and with some give and take you will achieve your goal. The world is full of compromises and this is one of them. In order to be able to accomplish that without too much stress, take some time and practice this Mudra to achieve absolute mental calm and focus. Clearly select a happy middle route to keep everyone happy and still arrive where you want to. Be tactful and play the game to win. Later, your compromises will become smaller and when you succeed on a large scale, everything may be done your way.

CHAKRA : All

COLOR: All

MANTRA:
**GOBINDAY, MUKUNDAY,
UDAARAY, APAARAY,
HARYNG,KARYNG,NIRNAMAY, AKAMAY**
(Sustainer, Liberator, Enlightener, Infinite,
Destroyer, Creator, Nameless, Desireless)

Sit with a straight spine. Place your hands at solar plexus level in front of you and interlace the fingers backward with palms facing up. Fingers are pointing up and the thumbs are straight.

BREATH: Long, deep and slow.

MUDRA FOR
POWERFUL INSIGHT

You are highly creative and love being in constant and ongoing project mode. Centre stage is right at home for you and you will easily acquire an enthusiastic and loyal audience. Organizing a large scale event or place of business is something you can tackle since you have a tremendous capacity for seeing the big picture. Your eyes are set on the highest prize and you make that clear. However, you motivation is the creative process and not pure ambition. The key to your achieving all and more than you ever desired, is to be be able to take some time and reassess the proper steps to get there. This may require you letting another person take over some aspects that they do better. Be open to equal collaborators and show flexibility. This will become your asset and make you unstoppable and undefeated. The best leaders are superbly clever with their warriors, they do not do everything themselves. Carefully select your "army" and watch your dreams become a reality.

CHAKRA: 6

COLOR: Indigo

Sit with a straight back, elbows out to either side. Raise your hands until they meet above the navel point. The back of the left hand rests in the right palm and the thumbs are crossed, left over right.

BREATH: Long, deep and slow.

MUDRA FOR BETTER COMMUNICATION

You know what you want and there is no doubt about it. However, some people may not be as capable, savvy and fast in following your direction. This is the time you can become bossy, patronizing and intolerant. It does not make the process easier, it only creates tension and unnecessary conflict. Stay focused, calm, and truly concentrate on remaining a good, pleasant, kind and respectful communicator. You are very loving and will attract loving people into your life that may feel hurt when you fail in proper communication with them. You can do anything you set your mind to, so this is one of those things-become a role model in diplomatic and harmonious communication and see the positive results manifest.

CHAKRA : 1, 2

COLOR: Red, orange

MANTRA:
RAA MAA
(I Am in Balance Between the Sun and the Moon,
the Earth and the Ether)

Sit with a straight spine. Connect the index and thumb fingers, creating a circle. Stretch out the rest of the fingers and rest your hands, palms facing down on your thighs or elevated in front of you. Hold for three minutes, breathe and relax.

BREATH: Long, deep and slow.

ABOUT THE AUTHOR

SABRINA MESKO **PH.D.H.** is an International and Los Angeles Times bestselling author of the timeless classic *Healing Mudras - Yoga for your Hands* translated into fourteen languages. She authored over twenty books on Mudras, Mudra Therapy, Mudras and Astrology, Holistic Caregiving, Spirituality and Meditation techniques.

Sabrina holds a Bachelors Degree in Sensory Approaches to Healing, a Masters in Holistic Science, a Doctorate in Ancient and Modern Approaches to Healing, and a Ph.D.H in Healtheoloyy from the American Institute of Holistic Theology. She is board certified from the American Alternative medical Association and American Holistic Health Association. She has been featured in media outlets such as The Los Angeles Times, CNBC News, Cosmopolitan, the cover of London Times Lifestyle, The Discovery Channel documentary on Hands, W magazine, First for Women, Health, Web-MD, Daily News, Focus, Yoga Journal, Australian Women's weekly, Blend, Daily Breeze, New Age, the Roseanne Show and various international live television programs. Her articles have been published in world-wide publications. She hosted her own weekly TV show educating about health, well-being and complementary medicine. She is an executive member of the World Yoga Council and has led numerous international Yoga Therapy educational programs. She directed and produced her interactive double DVD titled *Chakra Mudras* - a Visionary awards finalist.

Sabrina also created award winning international Spa and Wellness Centers and is a motivational keynote conference speaker addressing large audiences all over the world. She is the founder of Arnica Press, a boutique Book Publishing House. Her mission is to discover, mentor, nurture and publish unique authors with a meaningful message, that may otherwise not have an opportunity to be heard. She is the founder of world's only online Mudra Teacher and Mudra Therapy Education, Certification and Mentorship program, with her certified therapists spreading these ancient teachings in over 27 countries around the world.

www.SabrinaMesko.com

Made in the USA
Coppell, TX
01 September 2023